This book belongs to:

....

Written and edited by Josephine Southon
Designed by Claire Cater and Jack Clucas
Cover design by Angie Allison and Claire Cater

With special thanks to Betsy Bradley, aged six
and a half, for being a brilliant puzzle tester

MY HIDE AND SEEK
PUZZLE BOOK

Buster Books

First published in Great Britain in 2020 by Buster Books,
an imprint of Michael O'Mara Books Limited, 9 Lion Yard,
Tremadoc Road, London SW4 7NQ

With material adapted from shutterstock.com

W www.mombooks.com/buster f Buster Books 🐦 @BusterBooks

Copyright © 2020 Buster Books

ISBN: 978-1-78055-691-8

1 3 5 7 9 10 8 6 4 2

This book was printed in May 2020 by Leo Paper Products Ltd,
Heshan Astros Printing Limited, Xuantan Temple Industrial Zone,
Gulao Town, Heshan City, Guangdong Province, China.

INTRODUCTION

In this book, there are cheeky characters for you to spot, count and match. Are you ready to meet them? All you need is a pen or a pencil, and you're set for lots of hide-and-seek fun.

You'll find all of the answers at the back of the book.

So, what are you waiting for? Grab your pens and pencils and let's get puzzling!

TROPICAL BIRDS

Each bird has lost **two** feathers – one from its body and one from its wing. Can you **match** each feather to the bird that it has fallen from?

FANCY FROGS

Can you spot which one of these
frog princes is the **smallest**?

JIG-SAURUS

Take a look at this dinosaur scene and circle
the **two** jigsaw pieces below that **match** the grid.

CHILLING OUT

These polar bears are hanging out in the snow.

How many polar bears are having a drink? _____

5

DEEP-SEA DIVING

Look at this busy deep-sea scene.

How many **seahorses** can you count? _____

How many **starfish** can you find? _____

MAGICAL MIX-UP

Four horses have sneaked into Wonderland and are hiding among the unicorns. Can you **find** them all?

PREHISTORIC PAIRS

Welcome to the prehistoric portrait gallery.
Each dinosaur has a twin, pictured in an identical
frame. Can you **match** the pairs together?

MONSTER MASH

Can you circle the **three** body parts in the jumble at the bottom of the page that **match** those on the three monster pals?

AT THE ALLOTMENT

This colourful vegetable patch is bursting with lots of yummy things to eat. Can you **find** these **patterns** in the grid below?

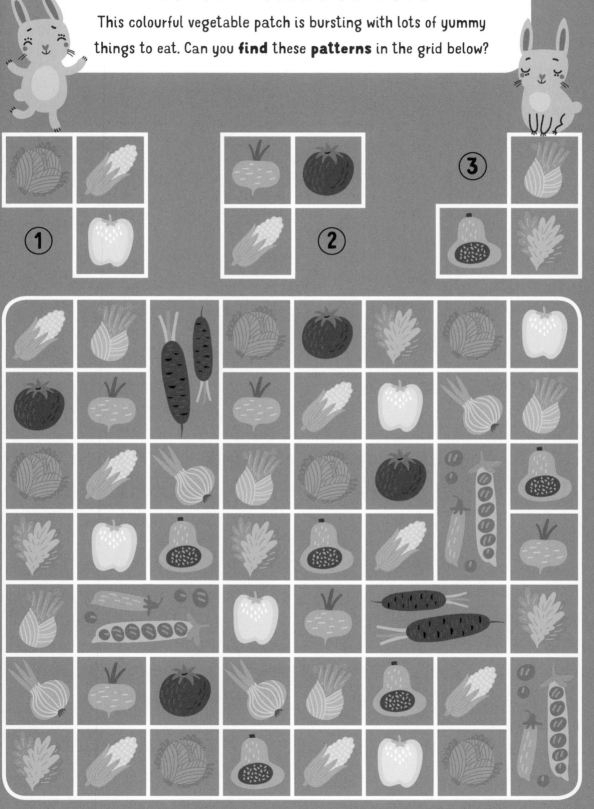

PUPPY PARADE

Within this crowd of puppy faces, there is an **odd one out**.
Can you find the dog that looks different to the others?

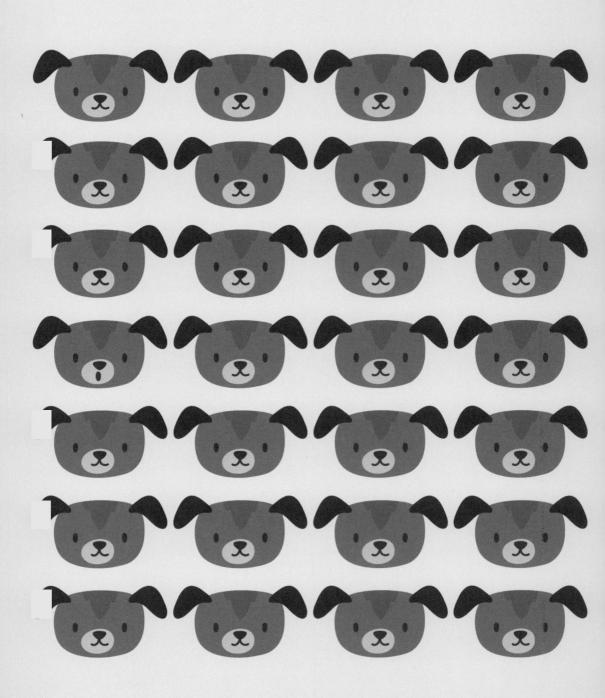

UP IN THE MOUNTAINS

Take a look at this jigsaw puzzle. Can you circle
the **missing piece** from the selection below?

CASTLE QUEST

As part of this knight's noble quest, he must make sure that there is **one** castle, **one** shield, **one** flag and **one** crown in each row and column. Can you help him by filling in the missing items?

PIRATE PAIRS

Ahoy there! Can you **match** each of these
shipmates with their silhouette?

RAINY DAYS

Three animals have lost their umbrellas in the storm. Can you work out which umbrella belongs to each animal?

1) **Percy's** umbrella matches the colour of Ralph's boots.

2) **Flip's** umbrella is the most colourful.

3) **Ralph's** umbrella is smaller than Flip's umbrella.

Percy

Ralph

Flip

GRIZZLY GAMES

These grizzly bears are playing their very own game of hide-and-seek. **How many** bears can you count sneaking around in the woods? _____

MOLE MAZE

Help this mole reach her family by following the underground tunnel. Can you **spot** and **circle** the following items on your journey?

· Wriggly worm · Pair of glasses · Sleeping rabbit

· Lost toy · Treasure chest

FINISH

PENGUIN PARTY

These penguins are having a party in the snow.
Can you spot a **polar bear** and a **seal**
who have popped along to join the fun?

DECK THE HALLS

Can you **match** each of these floating decorations
with those hanging on the Christmas tree?

AUTUMN SEARCH

When autumn arrives, colours of brown, red and yellow
can be seen all around you. **How many** acorns
and toadstools can you find in this picture?

Acorns _____   Toadstools _____

TRUCK TEASER

Can you circle the **three** parts at the bottom
of the page that are used in the panda's digger?

MINI MOUSE

Can you spot which of these
mice is the **smallest**?

BIRD-WATCHING

Imagine that you're looking out of your
window at these colourful birds.

How many birds have **red feathers** and **blue beaks**? _____

How many birds have **green feathers** and **red beaks**? _____

WILD BUNCH

Can you **find** these
patterns in the grid below?

①

②

③

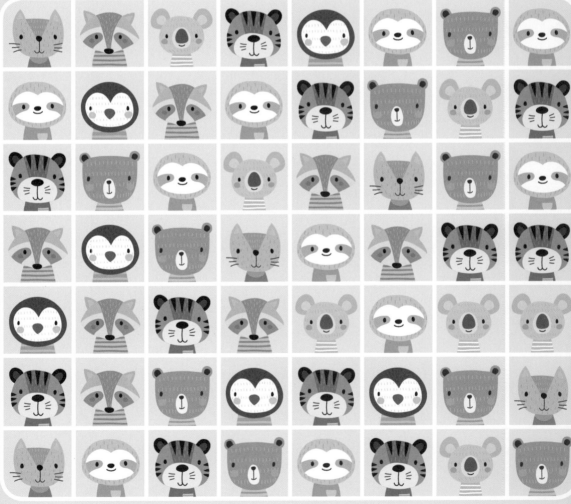

UNDER THE SEA

A deep-sea diver has taken two photographs
of this group of sea creatures. Can you
spot **six** differences between the pictures?

ANIMAL TOWN

Lots of happy animals live in this town.

How many **mice** can you spot? _____

How many **hedgehogs** can you find? _____

BITS OF BOTS

In the heap of metal at the bottom of the page, there are **three** pieces that **match** parts of this robot. Can you circle them?

DASHING DINOS

Look at these dinos run!
Quick, can you spot the **odd one out**
in each row as they speed past?

①

②

③

④

PLAYFUL POOCHES

Three children are looking for their dogs in the park.

Can you help them by following the clues?

1) **Ana's** dog is hungry for a bone.

2) **Lily's** dog has made friends with the smallest dog.

3) **Tom's** dog is looking at a dog with a blue collar.

Ana

Lily

Tom

WILD WHEELS

These critters are zooming off to a busy day at work.

Can you **match** each animal to its shadow below?

SLEEPY SHEEP

Can you complete the grid below, so that there is **one** moon, **one** cloud, **one** star and **one** sun in each row and column?

LET IT SNOW

These penguins like to wrap up warm in the chilly Antarctic weather. **How many** penguins are **not** wearing **scarves?** _____

GENTLE GIANTS

Can you spot which of these towering giraffes is the **tallest**?

SUNDAE FUN DAY

Can you **match** these ice creams into pairs?

Which **two** ice creams do **not** have an identical twin?

WOODLAND WANDER

Can you circle the **three** pieces that **match** the woodland scene on the opposite page?

ROAMING GNOMES

Can you **match** each one of these garden gnomes to its identical twin? Pay special attention to the colours of their outfits when you're pairing them up.

WHAT'S IN MY KITCHEN?

This kitchen is a mess!

How many of each of these fruits can you find?

Plums _____   Strawberries _____

Apples _____   Pairs of cherries _____

TRICK OR TREAT

Can you work your magic and spot **six** differences
between these spook-tacular scenes?

MONKEYING AROUND

It looks like this cheeky monkey got a little peckish.

How many fruits has he nibbled? _____

MONSTROUS MATCH-UP

Each of these kooky creatures has a terrifyingly identical twin. Can you **pair** them up?

JUNGLE JAMBOREE

Rehearsals are in full swing for this lively band.
Can you organize their music by making sure that there
is **one** of each symbol in every row and column?

COPYCATS

Some pesky **dogs** have sneaked in to pose among the cats.

How many dogs can you spot in the crowd? _____

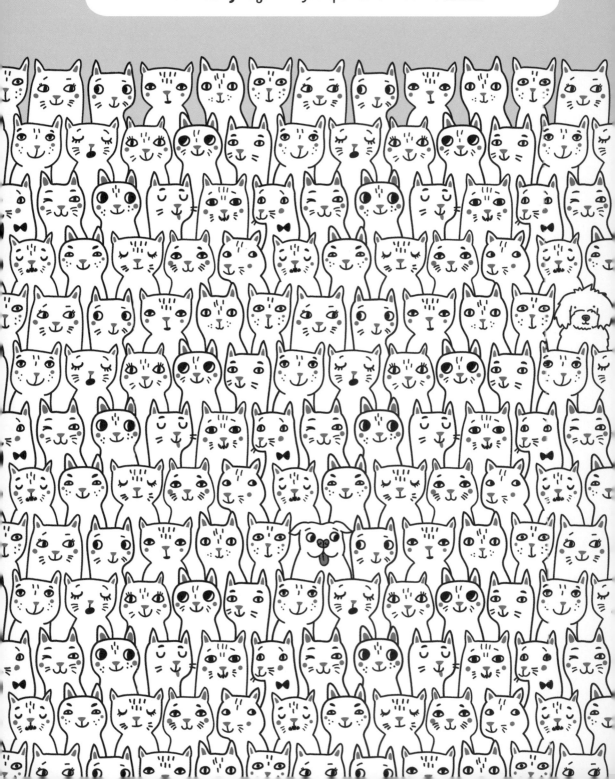

PARTY ANIMALS

Can you use the clues to work out
which present each mouse will receive?

1) **Minnie's** present matches the colours of her hat.

2) **Mildred's** present is tied with the thickest ribbon.

3) **Mark's** present is bigger than Mildred's.

Minnie

Mark

Mildred

NATURE TRAIL

Help big bear find his way home by following the woodland path.

Can you **spot** and **circle** these items on your way?

· Baby bear · Scarf that matches big bear's hat · Trail of pawprints
· Owl in a tree · Fish swimming in the river

START

FINISH

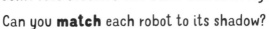

ROBOTS IN SPACE

Robots come in all shapes and sizes.
Some ride scooters and some can even fly.
Can you **match** each robot to its shadow?

ONE OF A KIND

If you look really closely at this family of dinosaurs you might see that one does not look the same as the rest. Can you find the **odd one out**?

CHASING BUTTERFLIES

Fred and Chip love butterflies and their beautiful colours.

How many butterflies have **red bodies** and **purple wings**? _____

How many butterflies have **blue bodies** and **pink wings**? _____

WHERE'S MY BABY?

Six baby animals have gone walkabout in the woods.
Can you **match** each parent to their baby?

COOL CATS

Take a look at this group of cats. Can you **find** these **patterns** of cheeky faces in the grid below?

SQUIGGLY SNAKES

Snakes can bend and twist their bodies into different shapes.
Can you **match** these snakes into identical pairs?

A TEAM OF TIGERS

Among this group of terribly cute tiger cubs
there is an **odd one out**. Can you spot it?

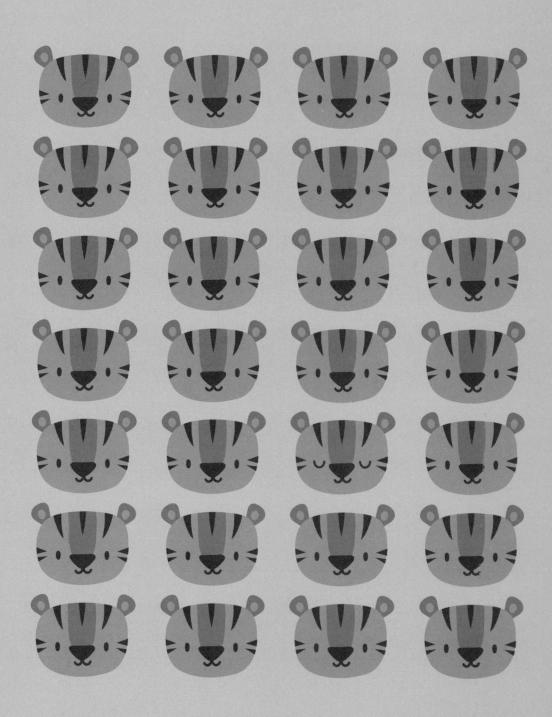

MONSTER MIX-UP

These wacky monsters are posing for a group photo.
Can you spot **six** differences between these pictures?

ONE, TWO, BEE

Bees love to roam around flowers collecting food. **How many**
busy, buzzing bees can you count on this page? _____

PRICKLY PAIRS

Can you **match** these cacti into pairs?

Which **two** plants do **not** have an identical twin?

SUMMER HOLIDAY

Can you use the clues to help these jetsetters find their luggage?

1) **Leon's** luggage has the most stickers.

2) **Timmy's** luggage is underneath the smallest bag.

3) **Snap's** luggage has wheels and is to the left of Leon's bag.

Snap　　　　Timmy　　　　Leon

CHEERY CHICKS

Can you **match** up **three** eggs on the grass with
three identical-looking eggs in the basket?

FUN AT THE FAIR

Help this bunny find her koala friend by following the trail.

Can you **spot** and **circle** these items on your journey?

• Little mouse • Bicycle-riding bear • Bird wearing a top hat
• Dog-shaped balloon • Bucket of popcorn

START

FINISH

SLOPE SCENE

Take a look at this snowy scene. Can you circle
the **two** pieces that do **not** match up?

MEOW-MAIDS

Can you **match** these magical mer-cats into purr-fect pairs?
Which **two** mer-cats do **not** have an identical twin?

MARCH OF THE ELEPHANTS

Elephants are the largest animals on four legs. Can you spot which one is the **biggest** of this bunch?

LOST IN SPACE

Using your puzzle skills, can you complete this cosmic grid so that there is **one** planet, **one** alien, **one** star and **one** rocket in each row and column?

BUG DETECTIVE

A magnifying glass helps you to see really small things, like bugs. Can you **match** the pairs? And can you find **one** bug that is **not** part of a pair?

FUNGI FIELD

You're out for a walk in the park.

How many mushrooms are **red** with **white spots**? _____

How many mushrooms are **purple** with **yellow spots**? _____

SAFARI SCHOOL

These book-loving buddies are ready for a day at school.
Can you **match** each animal to its silhouette?

LOTS OF LOOKALIKES

A cunning **cat** and crafty **bear** are trying to blend in with this crowd of bunnies. Can you **spot** them?

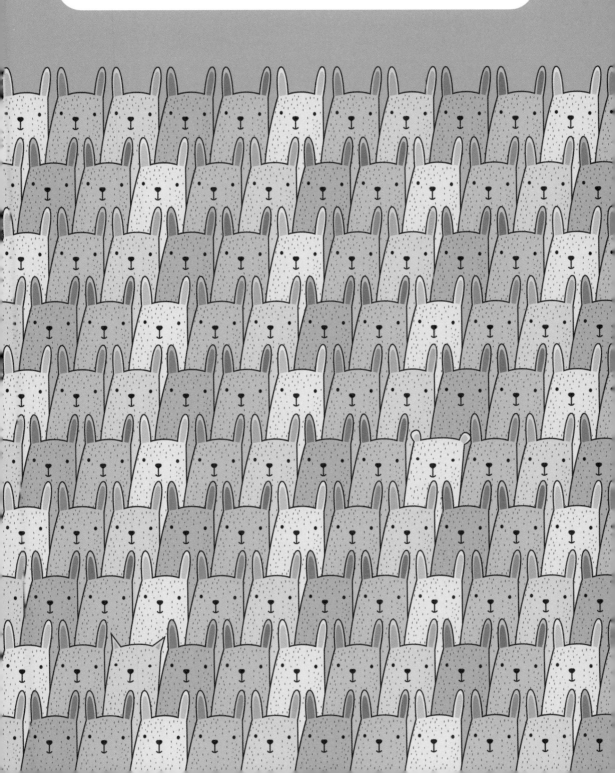

HOME SWEET HOME

These birds are trying to find their way home. Can you guide
each of them to the correct birdhouse by using the clues?

1) The **pink bird's** house is next door to a house with a red roof.

2) The **yellow bird** lives in the smallest house.

3) The **green bird** lives to the right of the yellow bird.

PEEKABOO

Can you **spot** each of these animals
sneaking around animal town?

CREEPY CRAWLIES

Take a close look at this group of bugs among
the flowers. Can you spot **five** differences
between the two pictures?

FELINE FRIENDS

Some of these playful kittens have lost their collars.

How many cats are **not** wearing **collars**? _____

ALIEN SIGHTINGS

Can you **match** each of these **six** aliens to their home planet by looking closely at their patterns and colours?

DUVET DAY

Can you **spot** these **patterns** on the cosy quilt below? Careful not to wake the sleepyheads!

ANSWERS

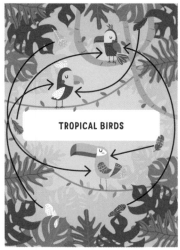

Puzzle 1

Puzzle 2

Puzzle 3

Puzzle 4

Puzzle 5

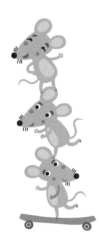

Puzzle 6

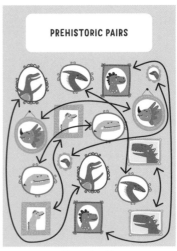

Puzzle 7

Puzzle 8

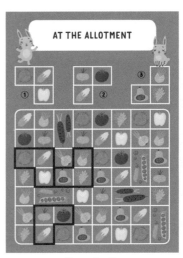

Puzzle 9

Puzzle 10

Puzzle 11

Puzzle 12

Puzzle 13

Puzzle 14

Puzzle 15

Puzzle 16

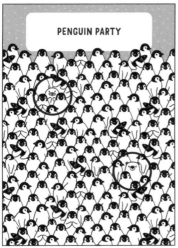

Puzzle 17

Puzzle 18

Puzzle 19

Puzzle 20

Puzzle 21

Puzzle 22

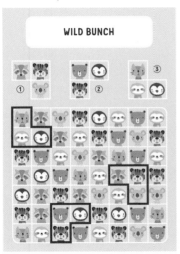

WILD BUNCH

Puzzle 23

UNDER THE SEA

Puzzle 24

ANIMAL TOWN
10 mice, 4 hedgehogs

Puzzle 25

BITS OF BOTS

Puzzle 26

DASHING DINOS

Puzzle 27

Puzzle 28

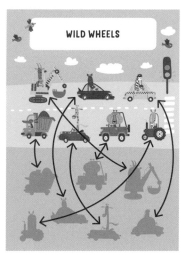

Puzzle 29

Puzzle 30

Puzzle 31

GENTLE GIANTS

Puzzle 32

SUNDAE FUN DAY

Puzzle 33

WOODLAND WANDER

Puzzle 34

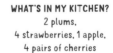

ROAMING GNOMES

Puzzle 35

WHAT'S IN MY KITCHEN?
2 plums,
4 strawberries, 1 apple,
4 pairs of cherries

Puzzle 36

Puzzle 37

Puzzle 38

Puzzle 39

Puzzle 40

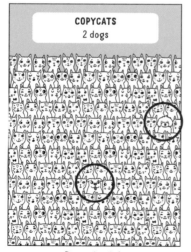

Puzzle 41

Puzzle 42

Puzzle 43

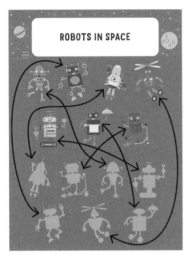

Puzzle 44

ONE OF A KIND

Puzzle 45

CHASING BUTTERFLIES
4 butterflies have red bodies and purple wings. 5 butterflies have blue bodies and pink wings.

Puzzle 46

WHERE'S MY BABY?

Puzzle 47

COOL CATS

Puzzle 48

SQUIGGLY SNAKES

Puzzle 49

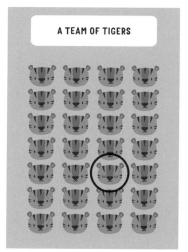

A TEAM OF TIGERS

Puzzle 50

MONSTER MIX-UP

Puzzle 51

ONE, TWO, BEE
10 bees

Puzzle 52

PRICKLY PAIRS

Puzzle 53

SUMMER HOLIDAY

Snap   Timmy   Leon

Puzzle 54

CHEERY CHICKS

Puzzle 55

FUN AT THE FAIR

START

FINISH

Puzzle 56

Puzzle 57

Puzzle 58

Puzzle 59

Puzzle 60

Puzzle 61

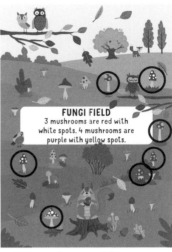

Puzzle 62

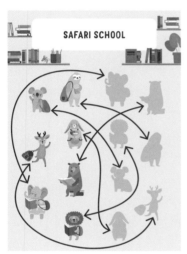

Puzzle 63

Puzzle 64

Puzzle 65

Puzzle 66

CREEPY CRAWLIES

Puzzle 67

FELINE FRIENDS
4 cats are not wearing collars

Puzzle 68

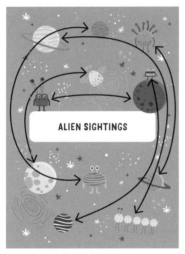

ALIEN SIGHTINGS

Puzzle 69

DUVET DAY
① ② ③

Puzzle 70